CW00865694

Church Path Publishing
Email: churchpathpublishing@hotmail.co.uk

Cover image © Eti Swinford

The Inner Sanctum

But you, when you pray, go into your
inner room, and when you have shut
your door, pray to your Father who is
in secret, and your Father who hears
in secret will reward you.

Matt. 6:6

One

When I shut myself off from external noise, clear my conscious mind and listen to the silence within, I hear your quiet voice. Many people may find it impossible to believe I hear the voice of God. How can I convince others that my contact with you is genuine?

You cannot. I have been communicating with creation from the very beginning, but there are those who refuse to listen even when they beg to hear my voice.

Surely that's a contradiction.

Of course. To understand the contradiction you must first accept the obvious confusion in the minds of those who will question the authenticity of your conversation with me.

I'm sorry, but you have already lost me.

All right. Let us start from the beginning. You desired this conversation for the purpose of helping your fellow beings at a time of considerable distress and confusion about the way forward.

Yes.

Did you have difficulty contacting me?

No, quite the opposite.

We are apparently going to discuss matters of some importance to you, yet your first question is how will others be convinced you are speaking with me. Is it not enough that you are speaking with me?

Yes. I'm just amazed that it was so easy to speak with you . . . . I'm overwhelmed.

Remembering what you just said you may now begin to understand the apparent contradiction in my opening response. What could be simpler than to be in touch with yourself? You are aware of changes within your fleshly body, every sensation and pain. You know that your fleshly body is merely an instrument enabling you to function in your present environment. You also know you are part of a vast universe created by me. You and the whole of creation are a vital part of me. You are aware of that are you not?

Yes.

Then how can any part of my self be out of contact with me?

Except by choice?

Yes. Now do you understand the contradiction caused from confusion?

I think so, but why has it happened?

Through separation. You can separate yourself from me in the same way that you can separate yourself from part of your body, say by amputation. That part of your body will wither and die if it remains separated.

But that would be harmful. If I am a vital part of you then why would you allow me to be harmed?

There are two answers to your question. In the first place you assume that amputation is harmful and I should prevent it from happening. This is a misunderstanding. I already said that your physical body is an instrument to enable you to function in your present environment. Your physical body fulfills a specific function as part of creation. The physical body is not the vital part of me I mentioned. Your body will perish as much of creation will perish in the continuing process of evolution.

But it is written that we were created in your image.

The second answer to your question is free will. You and the whole of creation are, as I said, a vital part of me. We are therefore of the same essence. You are as much of me as I am of you. As I have free will to create life, you also have free will to continue the process of my creation. Free will implies, indeed is, freedom to make choices. In your present environment you can choose to place yourself in positions which threaten physical amputation. This would cause you much pain, distress and suffering. However it is not life threatening. No amount of pain or suffering that is experienced in your environment is life threatening. It will be helpful for you to understand that nothing can be life threatening since I have not created anything that can be harmful to myself.

If I receive a fatal wound I will die. And you're saying that if I remain separated from you I will also die. Either way, as I see it, I haven't a hope!

You are attaching what I say to your bodily existence. That part of me that is the essence of your being is eternal.

I'm not actually aware of the existence of your essence in me. I'm only aware of my physical, emotional and mental existence and that's the part I'm most concerned about.

You do not know your own mind. If you were not aware of my essence in you then you would not have asked me to converse with you. You are sharing a similar difficulty with much of mankind. You want to believe in me but lack sufficient proof of my existence to silence your doubt.

You don't find that strange?

No. Doubt is always partner to free will. Free will demands reason, and reason cannot be exercised without doubt.

Do you mean that in giving us free will you expect

us to doubt your existence?

Yes.

Why? Is it some kind of test? Are you playing games with us? It seems to me you're deliberately laying traps that we're bound to get caught in.

Creation cannot be completed by robotic machines. No human being can conceive of the task before you. No man can comprehend the scale of creation or the ultimate purpose of evolution. My essence, that is the eternal part of you and every living thing in creation, must be able to continue the process of creation in my image; therefore all sentient beings must possess free will, otherwise creation could not continue.

That brings me back to the question of your image.

Can you see me?

No.

The reason you cannot see me is because I am not flesh.

Then what does it mean to say we were created in your image?

My image is life. Therefore everything in creation is evidence of my image. When you behold anything in creation, you are beholding my image. What your senses perceive as the material and ethereal world are elements of my image.

Man's ego developed and greatly inflated through the misguided belief that man alone was created in my image. This error is the source of separation from me and has contributed to my perceived remoteness.

I have always been taught that you were beyond the reach of any mortal.

You obviously did not accept that teaching.

It did not make sense. On one hand you were held up as a loving Father. On the other hand as a wrathful, vengeful God to be feared.

That belief suggests that I am flawed. That my creation is not perfect. It suggests I would punish those who others considered to be imperfect.

Would you not agree that life on Earth is far from perfect?

I certainly do not agree that life on Earth is imperfect.

From my point of view it seems imperfect. Never in my lifetime has the world been free of war, corruption and suffering brought about by the exploitation of man against man. More and more people take that as a sign you don't care. They argue that you do not exist. Even those with strong faith have been severely tested. Many felt deserted and are looking elsewhere for something to believe in.

Man's ego has always persuaded him to blame others when he has either failed to control or lost control of events. The history of mankind bears stark witness to terrible acts committed in my name. I cannot acknowledge what is not real.

Are you saying that human history is not real?

I am saying that nothing exists that I did not create. What you call imperfections do not exist in reality. It was correctly written that I made man simple. Man's complex problems are of his own devising.

They are very real to us.

Because human beings have imposed their own understanding to what is real. Your ego believes that it has a separate existence from me. It has convinced you that it is real. Ego does not exist. It has no reality. Your ego has assumed an illusion of reality, because outside of me it has no life. In order to sustain its apparent existence it has developed a thought system that is in conflict with me. It has argued that I do not exist; whereas the ego does exist. Indeed the ego, if you will be convinced of its truth, has more power over creation than I.

If what you say is true then why not reveal the truth and destroy ego?

You are not listening. I told you that ego does not exist, because I did not create it. How could I correct what does not exist?

But you are talking about ego as if it was an entity.

I am talking about something that is imagined to be real by a small part of creation. Every part of creation is one with me and has power to create with me in fulfilment of their specific purpose. My purpose cannot be achieved if individual creative powers were denied. Creation is an ongoing act of giving. It is not my purpose to impose my will on creation, but to give my power to all of creation in the certain knowledge that my purpose will ultimately be fulfilled. It may help you to understand when I say that I am powerless to do anything other than create.

Are you saying you have no choice?

I will to create. I have no will other than to create.

But you are God. You can do what you like.

Then in your terms, I like to create life.

I don't get it.

You apparently want me to say that since I create life I can also take it away. That if I dislike something I created I will destroy it.

Well something like that. You can, can't you?

Do you think I am mad?

Of course not.

Would it not be mad to create something precious and then destroy it?

I've always thought so. I have never understood why we destroy things we created with such loving care and great effort.

Is that not part of mankind's tradition?

Yes, but that doesn't make it right. Do you think wanton destruction is insane?

There are degrees of insanity. Not many human beings would regard war as a form of insanity.

Do you?

I can only create. Anyone who creates in my image is in my mind.

If someone is deliberately destructive does that mean he is out of his mind?

Anyone who is not in my mind will not be in their right mind. Therefore he will not be completely rational. To me that person will simply be in error.

Every error is capable of correction.

Are you saying you will forgive anyone who errs?

Forgiveness is a human practice. I have no need of forgiveness. There is nothing for me to forgive since nothing exists that would require forgiveness.

What about sin?

Sin is an invention of mankind.

But what about the original sin of Adam and Eve?

An allegory conceived by men.

Evil?

Evil is the ultimate degradation of ego.

You're turning my religious teaching completely upside down.

Would you like to terminate this discussion?

No. But are you really God, the Father and Creator of the Universe?

You will believe what you choose to believe. If you do not wish to accept my answers to your questions then that is a matter for you. I cannot frame my answers to suit preconceived ideas or errors of

10

teaching. If you want your thoughts to be confirmed then be content with books written by others in my name.

Is the Bible your Word?

My word is spoken to all as it is to you. Every part of creation need merely to ask to receive my word. Anyone who receives my word is free to make a record of what was said, but everyone has a different need and will hear differently from the next. Not everyone hears with the same ears or possesses the same mental state. He who has ears to hear with and a heart to understand what he hears will know the truth of what he has heard. One truth will not be heard the same by all who hear it. Anymore than one vision seen by multitudes will be interpreted the same by all people.

I am becoming very confused. Will you please help me to clear my mind so it can understand what you are telling me?

I know what is in your mind through my spirit that resides in you. Neither I nor my spirit can force your mind to accept my will. Whenever you ask you will receive. But you must understand that I cannot give whatever you ask if what you have asked is harmful. You can harm yourself, but I cannot respond to any request that might harm any part of creation. I will that all confusion be cleared from your mind and you hear and understand through your spirit what has always been yours to receive.

You seek for purity of mind and understanding in order to continue the purpose for which you were created. I embrace you, my son, and am pleased to enlighten you. You will not be confused by what I tell you. Your mind and body are one with your spirit and your spirit has always been one with me. You will rest and be lifted up by gentle forces into a universal mind that is beyond human understanding. I am taking your mind into mine and will return it to you when you possess the understanding you desire. Are you ready to come with me?

Yes, my Lord.

And so it is. You are now one with me and will know all there is to know about the thoughts and questions you have asked many times without knowing the answers.

Two

Father? This afternoon my wife and I spent a few hours at a Christian Center for Healthcare and Ministry. Shortly after returning home I felt prompted to read again, with a fresh mind, the conversation we had ten years ago. Ten years, Father. So little achieved in ten years. You said you would take my mind into yours and return it to me when I possessed the understanding I desired. I am chastened. I seem to lack understanding and am more confused than ever. I'm sorry. Either I failed to listen, or my mind did not retain what you put there. What's more I don't feel as if I stayed close to you.

There is no need for you to feel contrite. Allow me to put matters into perspective. Men of science have reasoned that the universe began approximately fifteen billion years ago. Every school child knows that measurement refers to the distance light travels in one solar year at a speed of 186,282 miles per second. A light year equals $5,878 \times 10^{12}$ miles, or 63,240 astronomical units. 3.262 light years approximates one parsec.

I wasn't taught that at school. What is a parsec?

A unit of measure for interstellar space equal to a distance having a parallax of one second as measured from diametrically opposite points on the earth's orbit. A megaparsec equals one million parsecs. Some galaxies are three thousand megaparsecs distant. Can you calculate in earth years when the universe became manifest?

I'm not Albert Einstein or Stephen Hawking!

Very amusing. Cosmologists are close but they cannot know the complexity of processes leading up to what has been called the Big Bang—the moment my thought erupted into life—as perceived by humankind. It is not yet understood that life actually began long before the universe was conceived. Ten earth years are little more than a rapid heart beat of a small star. Does that help to ease your mind?

Not a lot. You make ten earth years sound like the twinkling of an eye.

And so it is, relative to some star systems. You think you achieved little in your ten years. Not so. You cannot know what you have achieved since you cannot measure the effect of your thoughts.

Are you encouraging me?

If you wish to think so. I am simply saying that you should not judge yourself harshly. It will be beneficial if you keep your heart open to me and put your over active mind at rest.

That is not easy to do. My mind is constantly on the move. It never stops.

And so it is with most of your species. It is time for you to help others understand what you are becoming more aware of.

That is interesting. Some confusion disappeared the moment you put my concern over ten earth years in proper perspective. I am beginning to understand the relevance – or otherwise – of time. My species are enslaved by the concept that every second is precious and must not be wasted in idleness. We must be productive during every waking moment of the day and night in order to succeed. We exhaust ourselves in a senseless effort to create more and more wealth.

Explain.

When I was in my teens I seemed to have different ideas from most of my countrymen. I mean, the Great American Dream was about getting rich. The greater your wealth, the more successful you were as a citizen. I was frequently reminded that anyone could become wealthy. The idea was great encouragement for people who arrived from other countries with few possessions but plenty of ambition. Anyone born in America could become president. The unspoken caveat was that only the rich could afford to mount a bid to run for the highest office in the land. If I'm not mistaken most of my countrymen still hold fast to the American dream. Not many realize their dreams. Most might retain the aspiration but will settle for less. A minority will go to any lengths to achieve their dream, never realizing or caring about the cost to themselves, their families or the health of the nation. By all accounts I should have had the same ambition but chose a different path.

Tell me why you chose a different path.

All right . . . At the age of ten or eleven I had an experience – a visitation – from an angel?

A guardian spirit.

Why did that make such a difference to my outlook?

You were given a glimpse of truth because you were in need and asked for help.

I don't remember asking for anything.

Your heart asked why you were wrongly treated by your father. Do you not remember?

Yes, I remember. But why did I not concentrate on securing the dream of most Americans?

You understood something that was in the mind of another person, but you did not read what he wrote until many years later.

You must mean Henry David Thoreau.

Go on.

He wrote, "Why should we be in such desperate haste to succeed and in such desperate enterprises. If a man does not keep pace with his companions, perhaps it is because he hears a different drummer. Let him step to the music he hears, however measured or far away."

Who introduced you to that quotation?

My wife. She gave me a delightful picture of a boy standing on a cliff overlooking a valley with a river winding through. The last two sentences were inscribed in the glowing sky above the valley which was surrounded by a silver mountain range. I still have the picture. Those few words seemed to resonate within my soul. I was comforted by them.

And when did she enter your life?

When I most needed to learn the true meaning of love. Thank you for sending her to me.

You acknowledge a divine gift. Do you recognize the gift you are to her?

I dearly wish that was true.

I can assure you it is. You have learned to love in preparation for sharing divine love with others. The world has long placed great value on the love of trinkets.

Trinkets?

Manufactured goods.

Oh. Right.

People everywhere, entire nations, are dedicated to the production and accumulation of manufactured goods as the only measurable value of worthwhile achievement. You and many others have a different vision – hear a different drummer – and must now sound a music of greater harmony, healing and enlightenment for a world that has long been shaded from the spiritual light that provides life.

With respect you have the wrong person. I'm nobody. My brain just isn't good enough for such an important task. It's one thing to appreciate and apply the thoughts of fantastic thinkers to my own small life, but there's no way I can lift this planet and everyone on it to higher standards of living.

What about the quality of life?

Are you asking me to get on a soap box and tell people they are barking up the wrong tree? That they really don't need all the wonderful toys they play with? People the world over want what my countrymen have, or what the rest of the world seems to think they have. America is the envy of the world. And millions of people hate what America has because they haven't got it and think they never will get it.

They'd like to destroy America and everything it stands for if they can't have the same. Frankly, I have some sympathy – but not a lot – with their animosity. I empathize with their suffering from lack of life's necessities. Their lack seems unnecessary and unjust. But few people outside America appreciate the degree of poverty widely suffered in my great country. There seems little awareness of the decline in community and national ethics. . . .

Are you finished?

I have only scratched the surface. My head is crammed full. Worst of all is the obvious and painful realization that all the brilliant minds have failed to resolve burning issues that threaten humanity. We have invented just about every gadget imaginable to make our lives easier and more comfortable – and there are more in the pipe line to improve on the best. Most life threatening diseases have been wiped out, apart from mutations. We have become experts at killing each other. We're masters at inventing more ingenious weapons of mass destruction. Push a button and, zap, there goes another rubber tree plant with a few million human ants.

What are you intending to do about it?

We survive very well on what little we have. You blessed us.

Not in that way.

Pardon?

You have not been blessed by a particular standard of living. You have not been blessed by accepting less than those you vociferously condemn. You have not been set apart from those who devote themselves to exploit others and the planet for personal gain. You have not been singled out to engage in verbal combat with enemies conceived in your mind.

But I understood you to say . . . .

You heard me say people and entire nations are dedicated to the production and accumulation of manufactured goods as the only measurable value of worthwhile achievement. You did not hear me criticize or condemn their devotion.

But, I thought . . . .

You heard me voice a fact, nothing more.

I'm sorry. I guess I wasn't listening properly.

You were listening well. You simply heard what you wanted to hear.

Oh, dear.

Yes. Now, are you prepared to think like a man, my son?

With your help.

No!

Very well. I am prepared to think with truth in the core of my soul. The eternal truth that resides in every soul.

Correct. Now tell me. What is the freewill vision lighting your soul?

May I take a short break to think on that one?

I'll be waiting.

~ * ~

Right. I recall you saying that creation is an on-going act of giving; that every part of creation is one with you; and it is not your purpose to impose your will but to give free will to all of creation. You also said that you will not, or cannot, interfere with free will actions of humans. Since you apparently take credit for setting creation in motion but at the same time refuse to act as referee and blow the whistle when there's been a foul or even an almighty catastrophe, I think it's a bit rich that you turn around and ask me what I intend to do about it all? What do you take me for?

You may not hear it but I'm laughing with great gusto.

That's nice. Perhaps you will be good enough to share the joke with me.

21

It's the irony.

So . . . ?

Can you remember my last remark ten years ago?

You said, quote, You are now one with me and will know all there is to know about the thoughts and questions you have asked many times without knowing the answers, unquote.

Good. Now what's the answer?

I'm waiting for you to answer me.

Are you saying we are no longer one?

I'm not sure. My brain is overloaded.

May I suggest you think with your heart rather than your brain?

I'll try. . . . Ah ha! Well, well, well. Now I'm laughing. Can you hear me?

Loud and clear.

The answer is – nothing. I am to do nothing about the physical world in which I temporarily reside. It is the responsibility of every individual to choose the path they tread or to alter course if they make a mistake. Were I to interfere with freewill choices of others then

I would be imposing my will. The moment I became one with you I lost the desire to impose my will on any other part of creation. Had I attempted to interfere in the lives of others I could not have become a son of God. Is that right?

Nearly.

Okay. Wait a moment. My soul mind is telling me that within the scope of my immediate environment I have your power to be who I truly am. It is through my thoughts, actions and deeds that your power is reflected through me – providing, of course, that everything I reflect is lovingly creative. As your son I have no choice but to exercise compassion for the whole of creation. Excuse me. I should have said I have no desire other than to exercise compassion for the whole of your creation.

Our creation. When my children decide to return home we then truly are One.

You brought tears to my eyes.

Welcome home, my child. Welcome home.

Three

Father?

Here I am.

I'm in deep trouble.

Explain the conflict.

I don't know that I can. It's contradictory and totally confusing.

I already know.

In that case will you please sort it out for me?

It will help if you articulate your thoughts.

It's too painful. I want to finish with it. I want out of this life.

Does it help to punish yourself?

Okay! If you already know my problems then you'll know the horrible conflicts within my mind and body not that long after you told me I was your child. I actually began to feel I was one with creation. I felt empathy with every solid form I saw and touched. I could almost feel the living molecules and atoms in all life forms, animate and inanimate. I could sense intelligent purpose in basic elements. I almost felt

24

complete unity with the whole of creation. It was an amazing experience. Humbling. I felt like I was disappearing. As if I was blending in with everything else. Well, nearly everything else . . . everything but my own species.

That's when the rot began to set in. Whenever I observed the world created by my species, their goals, thoughts and deeds, I got more and more depressed. I wanted to do something, then remembered that I wasn't supposed to impose my will. I wasn't supposed to do anything. Unfortunately, that didn't stop me feeling the pain of others I passed on the streets or saw in café windows with blank, confused expressions on their faces. Mass media give the impression that people should strive for more and never be satisfied with less.

It seems to me that not one leader is prepared to recognize that increases in family breakdown, alcohol and drug abuse, mental illness, lawlessness and lack of respect for authority are direct results of lack of true and responsible leadership. They bang on about people taking responsibility for themselves, but too many of them are doing the complete opposite.

So what has your child done? Nothing, except turn to drink, become bitter in my heart and hurt the one person I love most. My humility turned to superiority. My compassion became disgust. My tolerance verges on hatred – mainly for my weakness and confusion. At first I was inspired by earlier conversations, began to feel self-righteous, then slowly began to doubt. I began to realize the unconscious thought behind my opening question to you, "Many people may find it impossible to believe I hear the voice of God. How can I convince others that my contact with you is genuine?"

My opening question should have been, "How can I trust or believe in you?" Everything I heard in my heart from you sounded right. Everything sounded true to my intuitive mind. My spirit was uplifted. I truly felt like a son of God. That is until human nature, once again, revealed its unpleasant side.

It would seem you do not have high regard for your species?

That's not so. I think we are the most brilliantly stupid species on planet Earth.

That is definitely a contradiction.

And in my opinion human beings are the most complex and contradictory species. Homo-sapiens are unbelievably talented and creative and inspiring. I wouldn't be depressed if I didn't know you were present in every single human being. I'm amazed at the miracles we perform, every single soul has the capacity to perform miracles. I think about the words of Jesus, "Truly, truly, I say to you, he who believes in Me, the works that I do shall he do also; and greater works than these shall he do; because I go to the Father." I naively expected the world to reflect that reality when I grew up.

What reality did you expect to find?

I thought we would be as attentive to every other

life form on the planet as we are to ourselves. We place self-interest above all else. I truly believed humankind would realize the obvious importance of maintaining proper balance in our relationship with creation. As long ago as 1854, Henry Thoreau wrote, "Nations are possessed with an insane ambition to perpetuate the memory of themselves by the amount of hammered stone they leave. What if equal pains were taken to smooth and polish their manners? One piece of good sense would be more memorable than a monument as high as the moon." That insanity prevails. Why? Why do we admire and quote from so many wise men, yet fail to incorporate their wisdom in the very fabric of our lives and enterprises? Why are we so lacking in common sense? I kept waiting for the evidence of good sense but was repeatedly disappointed. I kept expecting your image to be revealed in everyman.

My greatest disappointment surfaced from the realization that I, least of all, have been able to reflect your image or the wisdom of great men in my own life and attitudes.

Tell me about the dual reality you perceive?

What?

The reality of life on Earth as you see it.

Oh . . . . Well, my first memory was clinging to my father's back as he swam in the San Francisco Bay. My hands just reached around his neck enough for my fingers to lock. As I think about it, I was no more than a year old – if that – and he would have been in his mid to late twenties. My arms barely reached around his neck. I must have been very small. I wasn't frightened. It was exciting. From then on I slowly became aware of different, changing realities.

At what age did these different realities begin to appear to you?

I can't say exactly. It happened gradually. Probably when I began to be aware of the existence of things beyond my own body. Perhaps floating in water on my father's back was a pleasant shock that told my mind there was a huge reality beyond my small body.

Apart from my mother and father, there were two other boys in the house, my elder brothers. Other people started coming into my life. They turned out to be grandparents and other relatives and friends of my father. I was no longer the center of attention.

Continue.

As I became more aware of my surroundings it was necessary to adapt to changes that quickly overtook my perceptions. A simple example: infancy was problem free. I was regularly fed, bathed, changed and cuddled. It was a delightful period in every sense. However the atmosphere began to change as I grew. The peace and comfort I had earlier known was invaded by angry voices made by my parents and even my brothers. Angry voices were often accompanied by physical violence. I had to develop a form of self-defense. I developed a method that would hopefully distract their anger. I'd try to make them laugh.

I began to realize that I was born into a reality that was created entirely by other people. Everything – I mean everything in my life was created by someone else. The house I lived in, the furniture, my clothes, the food we ate and drank. There wasn't one thing that I created . . . that is, until I made my first model airplane and stuff like that. Even my models were designed and manufactured by others. I simply stuck them together. But the point is this, my entire life has been carefully orchestrated and conducted according to arrangements made by others. I have literally been a passive witness to be manipulated by all and sundry who knew the right strings to pull. I don't know how many times we mentioned free will during these discussions but a valid description of my free will is simply following the herd wherever it led.

So long as my needs were served, and most of the time I had absolutely no notion what my needs were or how best they might be served. I was like a puppet with no conception of what life was all about or my purpose in life. However at some point in my youth I knew I couldn't survive without paying others for the privilege.

I am tired of being manipulated by my species, of being in total bondage to economic and social systems created by the brightest of our species. The one and only element on this planet to which men have not yet been able to claim ownership is the air we breathe. How they would love to own that!

Soothsayers have long been shunted into wasteland sidings. Wealth creation is the mantra on the lips and in the minds of all the great and good. And who, we may ask, will not bend to the will of the great and good? I reasoned that since You gave us free will, who can say my species have not chosen the correct path in the course of evolution? If the purpose of life, according to human consensus, is wealth creation then who can say that is not a worthy interpretation? If I choose to follow the herd into the abyss, so what? That would be the result of my freedom of choice. It was a gift from You. How can You then judge my decision, given the fact that I freely exercised my personal will?

Are you calm enough to listen?

What's your answer?

Firstly, you have already judged yourself. Turmoil and confusion were allowed to enter your mind. You exercised free will and became separated.

That's the whole point! I'm a human being!

So am I.

What? What are you saying? How can you be human? How can you know what it's like to suffer the agony that's dished out every moment of the day and night?

As creator of all that is, was and ever shall be, I exist in every animate, inanimate and ethereal entity that exists throughout the cosmos. Human beings are the most creative and intelligent species on Earth. Human beings are a direct result of the eternal process of evolution and, similarly with all of creation, are of my essence. You are becoming a reflection of your creator.

Right. You told me that nothing exists that you did not create. Well, if you're human, you'll know what we earthly humans are doing to this planet and to ourselves is ultimately wasteful, egocentric and destructive. If you are human, then why are you blind to what's going on here? Are you deliberately ignoring the realities experienced by flesh and blood humans? Are you blind to the genocide, corruption, insanity, exploitation, cruelty and inhumanity in every human society? Are you insensitive to physical and emotional suffering we experience almost daily? The pain is real! We feel it in every fibre of our being. It twists our bodies and minds into agonizing shapes. We turn to drink and drugs and anything to ease our pain. Every pleasure of the flesh and mindless brain is readily available. After all, those pleasures are great wealth creators.

We have cast our brilliance aside and willingly become increasingly mad . . . insane . . . in pursuit of what you say doesn't exist because you didn't create it. Frankly I think that's a cop out. I think you have been misleading and selectively avoiding acknowledging a reality that exists; one, albeit, created by human beings. If you are one with all life created by you then it sounds false to say nothing exists that you did not create. You created us and we created the world in which we live. We created the systems controlling our lives. We

31

created conditions that affect the lives of other species. We created weapons of mass destruction and use them to destroy others. We have literally become gods through our power to create and destroy as we choose. It deeply offends me to say this, but who needs you?

We cannot survive without each other.

How so?

If I did not exist neither would you. If you did not exist nor would I.

I assume you mean the entire universe.

Yes. Think about creative love. Think deeply about what it means to create through love. Ask yourself what has been created without love as its primary source of inspiration. Ask yourself how could I possibly not feel the pain you expressed. and more than you could endure.

(A surge of emotion made it difficult for me to speak)

Then allow your mind to contemplate how much love you will need to endure the pain of evolution from the beginning of everything. How could you survive and still be filled with love as the only power at your disposal? How could you endure pain without love?

(I felt as if my heart was being ripped open)

Repeat the closing lines of the story that was channeled through you.

"When you fully understand and confess that I can never desert you nor forsake you is when you will eternally be one with me. When you and all humankind choose life is when you will be released from inner strife. Do not worship me. Simply be as I am. Recognize and respect diversity within yourself, in others and the whole of Creation. In so doing you will learn that nothing exists apart from God. Recognition of that fact will enable you to see with my eyes. Through you others will see themselves more clearly, as I do, and will endeavor to reflect what you see rather than imposed or acquired distortions. There is nothing to worship, but everything to encourage, respect and embrace in the glory of Creation."

You have memorized the words. Allow them to become your sole reality. Let the world see myself through you, so the world can see itself through my eyes. You will then know ecstasy through the pain of Love.

Amen. Thank you, Father.

Made in the USA
Charleston, SC
10 January 2015